I0586288

The Long Acre Paddock

A Memoir in Verse

LINDA RUTH BROOKS

GUM TREE press

Copyright: Linda Ruth Brooks © 2020
All rights reserved. This book is copyright protected. Apart from
any fair dealings for the purpose of private study, criticism,
research or review as permitted under the *Copyright Act
(Australia),* no part may be reproduced by any process without
written permission. Enquiries should be addressed to the
copyright owner.

ISBN: 978-0-6482869-9-8

A copy of this book can be found in the National Library of
Australia, Canberra

Cover & interior design: *LRB Publishing Services*

Photographs: author's own
Watercolour artwork © Linda Brooks

Literary nonfiction/poetry/memoir

This book, and others by Linda Ruth Brooks, may be purchased
through amazon.com, author & online bookstores: Book
Depository, Fishpond and Booktopia.

Dedicated to my outstanding English teachers and University lecturers, Iris Yob, Arch Hefran, Rob Cooper, Moya Costello, Lynda Hawryluk, Iris Curteis and Nell Cook. All of whom possessed and taught a passion for the written word.

Take down the love letters from the bookshelf,
the photographs, the desperate notes,
peel your own image from the mirror.
Sit. Feast on your life.

Love after Love, Derek Walcott

Contents

LIFE

is
a slip
on the ice

It's a spent game
a try, a clash
a save, a dash

It's a burger
with the works
a song & dance,
a purloined chance
a flashy show,
a slow-river flow
a blind quest,
a fleeting guest

It's a dense mirror
a cloudy glass,
a quick pass
a heedless pawn,
a crystal dawn,
a sly ploy,
a heart-busting joy

It's a sinner's prayer

ONE SHOE OFF

I'm the kid with the curls
and the perpetual smile.
Mum said I drove her nuts that day
because one of my shoes kept falling off.
A fair summation of my life actually.

SILVER

I came into the world
around 3 o'clock
in the afternoon,
around the time schoolkids
were shouting with glee

and rushing home, glad
to be rid of the rules
and stricture of the classroom,
the tedium of learning
and the watchful gaze
of teachers.

I often wondered why
my mother remembered
the relationship to school times
whenever she recounted
the story of my birth. Education
was the path to success
in her eyes. She'd

longed for more of it for herself
so perhaps that explained it.

AN ECHO AWAY

If you followed
the slow, muddy creek,
you would follow me.
Follow my life.
the first bit anyway,
the growing up bit.

And after all, isn't that
the important slice?—
the part the rest
is framed upon?

Home is a promise,
a jerk, a prayer,
a flinch, a bust.
never more
than
an echo away.

We lived on a road
that followed the creek.
in three different houses
on that street. The top end,
the bottom end,
then the middle.

The first one
was the last house
at the north end, separated
from thick, dense scrub
by a barbed wire fence.

My brother, three years older,
constantly sought
to escape the confines of our yard
with repetitive determination.
Mum called him
"a blooming Houdini",
although his modus operandi
did not live up to that illustrious
reputation. He merely slipped
under the barbed wire and bolted
every chance he got.

Mum's solution
was equally repetitive
but less successful.
She later said,
I was forever tearing after the kid.
Scrambling through
barbed wire fences
with long floral skirts and aprons
was an altogether awkward affair.

Apparently I displayed
no desire to follow my brother,
but stayed close by
the clothesline making patterns
with Mum's pegs.

We lived on the creek, my brother
and I. He was variously:
Tom Sawyer,
a pirate or a warlord
leading troops.

The rest of us kids obeyed
like adoring slaves.

He appropriated
truck tyre tubes. We drifted
in rafts on that silty old creek,
swung from high ropes or gouged
thick sludge from the creek bed
to throw at other kids.

We shared the bush track with cows,
wombats, snakes and strutting herons
that feasted on the riches
of the sludgy creek. It
was a muddy backdrop
to our childhood. Once
broad and flowing,
barges had travelled its length
carrying timber to the local mill.

While we lived there
violence intruded—
the owner of the corner garage
was gunned down by a man
refusing to pay for petrol.

Then, in America, some madman
with three names shot and killed
John Fitzgerald Kennedy
on my ninth birthday.
I refused to eat the Dolly Varden cake
Mum had made and ran outside.
You can't cry for everyone Mum said.

Dad found me and held me close,
soothing me against his rumbling chest.
I ranted and railed.
The world had gone crazy.

We kids played at war, having
our own rules—'don't get up
until you count to ten when you've
been shot dead'. There was
no counting
for Mr Strong, the garage owner.
There would be
no counting
for John Fitzgerald Kennedy.
I never played at war again.

I climbed up into the tree-house
and lay on the rough uneven timber.
I moved behind the beams
so no one could see me,
and stared at the sky
through the branches
of the mulberry tree.

I watched the clouds
scud across the milky sky
and traced the patterns
of the shadows
made by the November sun
as they fluttered around me.
I didn't want to go back
to the mess of life.

I stayed until the crickets' song
began its staccato chorus.

When the chill of the evening air
waved across the acre paddock,
furling the long dry grass
I heard Mum call.

I scrambled down
the crooked paling struts
that formed a rough ladder
down the tree trunk. That night
I dreamed I lived up in the tree tops
with nothing but the curded sky
and the dimpling
of the ponderous creek
for company.

At school, my brother decked
anyone who laid a hand on me,
coming out of nowhere like Zorro,
and leaving just as quickly.

We watched the townsfolk
the vagrant, the sly drunk
the housewives gossiping
over fences, twitching their hands
to hide whispered secrets.

They're all gone now.
My parents, my brother.

The widows, the aunts,
the working men
and all the miscreants
of my childhood—
the saccharin man with his lolly jar
for treating small girls,
the man who hid his whisky
hidden in the gnarled eucalypt,
the ancient bearded man who lived
under sky and moon and saw visions.
They're all drifting
in some other river of dreams,
another place.

I still dream of treetops and creeks,
cricket song and mulberry stains.
On pensive days when the breeze
furls the paspalum and a bleached sun
meanders across a milky sky,
I can almost hear my mother's voice
part the evening air—
Time for tea. Time to come home.

STRETCHED SUMMER DAYS

chill of cool water
kissing sting of sun
rain on tin rooftops
trees shade saltwater lakes
midnight phosphorescence

timeless space, wind-carved ravine
red-orange, blue-purple
tulle fuchsia-skirted bottlebrush
orange-velvet kangaroo paw
wax flower, cowslip orchid
flame grevillea, hooded lily

horizon sharpened
interrupted by ocean
endless white sand
washed-pale cerulean skies
joyful splash of wattle
eucalypts crowd shorelines
towns crouch on coastlines

red-brick sliced mountain ranges
flaunting dark green treed cliffs,
amber-bright dawns
Nullarbor dreaming greets treeless horizon
red dust meets turquoise dessert sky
grey-green low succulents

salt-washed beach grasses
children slide on cardboard sleds
down terraced sand dune

SHOES

(tales my mother told me)

shoes

thick card inserts

all the miles to school

poor protection from harsh winter chill

rough trail through scribbly gums

soles redone by father

frequently

BILLABONG

willow's trail
summer rain adorns
tear-stranded chains
in mud-brown waters
at creek's elbow
where once we played
on bleached summer days
giggling and hiding
within playful strands.
moss-slimed roots jut
from clay-bedded banks
their velvety strength
forged there,
fixed, resolute.
How forgiving the branches
as we clung and swayed
how easily they bent low,
persuaded,
to join our play
as we danced like water elves
singing summer's last song.

WATAGANS

fragrant pine needles
scrunch underfoot
clear mountain air tantalises
pine cones huddle
campfires crackle

memories scramble
for front row seats

in the forest
shadows add beauty

birdsong is phrased
by the echo of waterfalls
each a prelude to the next...

stone steps
rough hewn railing

sated we descent
the wishing well still waits
replete with my childhood coins

FIRST JOB

My first job
was at a roadside
vegetable stall.
          I was twelve.
I rode there on my pushbike,
weighed fruit and vegetables
shouted at by the crabby woman
who grew the vegetables.

I once got the price wrong
had two bob taken out of my pay.
It was obvious I'd inherited
none of my mother's talent.
a grocery store manager,
a mathematical genius with addition
subtraction and multiplication.

After high school, and
before nurse training
I worked at the local food cannery.
I slow off the mark, wrecked
things. I started
in some steamy room
packing sausages into tins.
I could never fit
the right number in.
No matter how I tried
the last one was always torn,
squished and had to be
thrown out. After a few days
of this malarkey

I was thrown out,
generously referred to as a
'transfer'. I was put
on the breakfast bix machine.

With expert fingers the line women
picked up 6 bix in each hand and
place them precisely in the boxes,

I picked six up in each hand
and broke the outside ones
four broken out of twelve
was not considered acceptable.

I was moved to the cornflakes line.
twelve women, six to a line. They were
not impressed with inept kids
fresh from school, they gave
no advice or assistance
but sat there scowling
or gossiping about their sex lives—
all this with a beady eye on me,
waiting to giggle at my discomfort.

I pretended to be deaf,
which didn't bother them much
when they were yakking,
but annoyed
the hell out of them
when they felt the need
to tell me what to do.

Six jobs per side—
1: Catch the cornflakes
out of the shute into a plastic bag
and place on conveyer belt.
2. & 3: are hazy – I probably
never caught on
4: roll down the plastic bag.
5: put the toy in.
6: Goodness only knows.

It was on No. 1 that I really stuffed up.
I only managed to catch 2 out of 3
on a good day. I didn't have
many good days. When you missed
the cornflakes flying out of the shute
they landed in a bin at your feet.

With my imprecise muddling
this had to be taken away often,
which meant both lines shut down.

While the women showed no interest
in efficiency and speed
to deliver more than necessary
they were appalled at my ineptness.
I told the foreman I couldn't keep up
with the machine and he sped it up. Great.
Now I was catching one in four.

I had watched how he sped the machine up
a few times and when he was gone
I opened the hatch and slowed it down.

The women gasped, but
I caught every single one then. However,
the machine, and thus all 12 women
were forced to speeds a snail
would be ashamed of. They murmured
and complained in Biblical fashion
so I hummed a very slow waltz.
Out of tune.

The foreman would return
and speed it up. I would slow it down.
It broke. They sent an electrician.
My brother. 'It was you, wasn't it, Sis,'
he said, as he set about fixing the machine.
It took half an hour.
I pretended to have a power nap.

As soon as he left I started again.
The foreman was suspicious, but
for some strange reason none
of the women told him what I was up to.
He glared at me when the thing
shut down the second time.
'He'll go and tell the big bosses,'
warned the women.

'Rubbish,' I said, 'you don't really think
he's going to go over to the office
and tell them a teenager
who's only been here a week,
worked out how to do his job?'

I was transferred to a far corner
of the factory where all that was required
was to pick the skins off peanuts
as they went along a conveyer belt. The
peanuts had already been tumbled
so there wasn't much skin left. It was here
that I discovered an unusual phenomenon.
Much like sitting a train—the train
next to you is moving, but it's hard
to tell what's moving and what isn't.

I was mesmerised. A friend came
and watched me. 'Hey, Brooks, you're not
getting many skins there. Those peanuts
are rushing past—you're missing 'em.'
'Ah,' I said, 'the peanuts aren't moving,
the machine is. Watch it long enough
that's what happens.'

My school nemesis was on the prowl,
she'd been working there two years
and was full of self-importance.
My ineptitude was her opportunity.
'Jeez, Silver. Not the dux
of the school here are ya?
You're completely useless.'

'I know,' I said, smiling generously,
'isn't it marvellous! I'm getting
paid the same as you but
I'm absolutely rubbish
at everything.

ACCIDENTAL FEMINIST & PART-TIME TYRANT

I'd skived school and was weighing
potatoes in the STAFF ONLY
packing and loading area
of THE TRADING & CO-OPERATIVE STORE,
known colloquially as THE CO-OP.

I made tedious work of this task,
choosing potatoes of varying size, putting
them on and off the scales, attempting
exactness, until Mum asked what the blazes
I was doing, then said. 'Just make sure
you're over. Always. Never jip people.'

Mum stood at the back of the store
eyes narrowed, hand on hips. After
a thoughtful *Hmmph,* that portended trouble
she headed for the front of the store.

'Jane's on the warpath,' said
a grinning shop assistant, grabbing
the sleeve of a workmate and pointing
at my mother's resolute back.
The prospect of relief from boredom
was irresistible so I followed.

Mum's straightforward brutality
on matters of work ethic was legendary.

She'd announced her promotion
to MANAGER with 'Let's see how
they cope with petticoat government'.

I peeped over the GENERAL CLEANING
aisle, pleased Mum had lowered the height
of the aisles to survey the activities
of 'thieving college students'.

A plump, stylish woman
had entered the store
and was removing her gloves.
She held a nondescript garment
wrapped loosely with tissue paper.
With head held high she scanned
the store, and waited.

'You can't bring that back.'
Mum's voice carried over the morning
crowd of customers. 'You'll
have to pay for it, or give it back.'

The woman stalled. A red flush
rose from her neck and spread. She
turned to face my mother, hands fisted.
Mrs Ellmore had a reputation too,
she was no shrinking violet.

The room fell silent with only
the chink of the cash register.
'I had this on *appro[1]*,' Mrs Ellmore said,
'approved by *you*. I'm returning it.'
'Appro is four days, not
"as long as you please"—you've

---

[1] "Appro" stands for Approval, a system where customers could take items
of clothing home to try on. Garments were taken on trust – there was no
payment at the time, until today's system.

had it for over a month.
Most people can ascertain if a garment
fits in five minutes, not five weeks.'

The woman stiffened.
'You do know who I am!'
This rhetorical question confused Mum
who lived in a black and white world.

'Don't be ridiculous, of course I do.'
Mum took the parcel, turned
on her heel and walked away.

Mrs Ellmore paused, then smiled
and glanced at the onlookers,
who developed a sudden interest
in the contents of their trolleys.

TOE TO TOE

Early in life
Mum and I had parried
over a million subjects.
Dad's assessment
was that neither of us knew
when to leave well enough alone.

He was, of course, right.
I began as a toddler with questions:
'Why can't my cat talk?'
'Does God wear pyjamas?'
'Who's in charge
of all the money in the world?'

When I was five
I walked into the kitchen
while Mum was mopping the floor.
This activity involved
vigorous swishing
that left streaks of water up the wall
and was accompanied
by loud thumping
as the mop hit whatever was in the way,
occasionally a miscellaneous child.

'Get off my clean floor, Kate!' she yelled.
'How many times do I have to tell you blasted kids.'

'But you're on it,' I said, facing
certain disaster. 'And your feet are bigger
than mine. Why do you walk over the floor

while you're mopping it anyway? If you started
at the other end you'd finish
in the laundry without walking over it.'

'Look at you, all of five,
telling me what to do.' She snorted
and gave me The Look—I'd seen
her use it on Dad often; the
"You're A Right Smart Arse" look.

When I was older my opinions
confounded her as much as my earlier questions.
I developed anti-royalist sentiments
that confused her. She revered
the monarchy. We sang *God Save the Queen*
at every function, local, church or school.

I told her God was not in favour
of the monarchical system. I read a text
from the Bible where God gave in
to the Israelites and let them have a King
like the heathens so they would learn
what a ridiculous idea the whole royalty gig was.

She was appalled. The only thing worse
than a smart arse was one with God on their side.

BILLY AND ME

I was named Kate, after my mother's favourite sister. They were the youngest of eight, separated from the others by illness and immaturity. Mum had Bright's Disease and was wrapped in blankets to sweat the fever out. She got over it. Aunt Kate had asthma and never got over it. Mum had me and Aunt Kate had Billy. We were so much alike we said we should've been twins. I had an older brother and Billy had a younger sister. Neither of them got us at all. We were both curious and chatted away like crickets, roaming around our back yards looking for treasure and creatures. My brother said we were like a toothache. We didn't care. We were five.

Our families didn't hug much. Billy and me ran round together, one arm around the other most of the time, giggling and looking. We hugged the world. Mum was never sick. Except when she had all her teeth out. Her mouth dribbled blood and nonsense when she came home from the hospital. Dad said the anaesthetic made her silly. It still worried me because she was never silly so I sat by her bed. She kept trying to get up, all wobbly and loose. I just stayed and put her legs back in the bed. Dad said I didn't have to do that, but I couldn't stop. Billy's mother was in and out of hospital, drowning for want of air to breathe. We were ten.

Mum became a shop manager and Aunt Kate took in sewing, piece work for a factory. Mum unloaded delivery trucks beside the men. They struggled to work as hard as she did. Some of them didn't like her much. She said it was because of petticoat government. Aunt Kate ran out of breath in the winter and died on the way to hospital. The next year Billy's father died and he came to live with us. One morning I got up and he was gone. His room was empty, not even a hint of him. It was as if I'd dreamed him. Mum tried to push on my leg in church so I'd kneel down with the congregation to pray. I slapped her hand away and told her she could have God all to herself. I was fifteen.

THAT KIND OF STREET

IT WAS THE KIND OF STREET where kids moaned that nothing ever happened, but not to their parents who took anything approaching whingeing as an opportunity to make lists of chores and threaten to get a petition for the government to bring back child labour.

IT WAS THE KIND OF STREET where any resident would protest that they never gossiped and deplored anyone who did. This claim, made over fences and gates, was usually followed by an objective critique of all persons who weren't present at the time.

IT WAS THE KIND OF STREET where curtains twitched and everyone knew what everyone else was doing, and quite possibly much of what they might do in the future. This involved a great deal of social manoeuvring where a good memory and a keen eye for random eavesdroppers who might break the careful rules of society by taking the tale back to the gossipee, which was a fate to be avoided at all costs because of the stress of the invention of the most acceptable white lies that would have to be told. Oh no, I said nothing of the sort. How could you think that of me?

IT WAS THE KIND OF STREET where kids became bored with scraping sticks, rolling tyres and swapping marbles, being bereft of PlayStations and iPads. This led to children to becoming excessively interested in listening in to adult conversation. Or it might have just been me. I found that contrary to populist claims, a whole lot of stuff happened, things that would make Days of Our Lives look a bit tame. If one was paying attention of course, or, hiding in the treehouse while mothers didn't gossip over the fence. All of this would be called network in the future.

IT WAS THE KIND OF STREET where a rotund church deacon took a constitutional after lunch to the other end of the street. Taking a detour to a knotty gum tree, he reached into a crevice, found his whiskey bottle and took a tipple or three. Local boys who knew of this habit often availed themselves of a tipple or three themselves, replacing the alcohol with water in a reverse miracle of The Wine At The Wedding. At the intersection the garage owner was shot dead with a sawn-off shotgun by a certifiable dimwit who drove to the nearest café where he was arrested halfway through his burger, and before he'd sampled his hot chips.

IT WAS THE KIND OF STREET that had a seldom used airstrip at one end where we hooned around in go-carts which I tried to convince my father had adequately prepared me to drive a car without lessons. He gave up. My then boyfriend, who was particularly adept at giving up, also gave up. Mum sent me to a driving instructor with a bad temper and deplorable manners, who called me a maniac if you please! There was the sibling incest that everyone for a fifty mile radius knew about and cheerfully passed on. Another deacon with pleasant manners passed around the offering bag for the tithe-paying parishioners, went home with his wife and children, enjoyed lunch then had a nap ... with his girlfriend on the other side of town. There was a car theft, a jail term, shooting of street lights. You see what I mean now, we're only up to the fifth paragraph and there's been adultery, alcoholism, theft, incest, vandalism and murder.

IT WAS THE KIND OF STREET that had an estimable cast of characters, enough to fill several Netflix sagas. An old white-bearded man who resembled a dwarf scared children by telling them he would eat their pets. His wife always wore an apron and could have easily stepped off the pages of a Dickens' novel. There were the dainty old ladies who toiled in their garden and were always ready for a chat or an impromptu sandwich. One old darling had a dining chair for her cat. There was the builder who promised to fix us kids up with a swimming pool if we dug the hole. We managed mere inches. There was the woman who tatted while her husband caught tadpoles. The mad bastard who took his rattling rusty wheelbarrow to the corner store for groceries and repaired a dent in his car door with cement that fell off halfway down the street. His wife shrieked and screamed every day as cats and rats escaped through long grass and then tall fences to face the neighbour's .303. There were businesses in residential zoning—an electrical appliance shop, a second-hand car yard and a mechanics workshop.

IT WAS THE KIND OF STREET where women collected Artex paints then covered aprons and tablecloths, attended tedious cycles of Tupperware parties until their kitchens contained little else. Mothers bought camphor chests and kitchenware for the daughters' glory boxes, encouraging their offspring to marry up and not down. Terrified of unwanted pregnancies they lectured through all the daylight hours with never a thought of providing anything by the way of the facts of life that went beyond the film put on at the church hall, narrated by an elderly bespectacled woman with dour demeanour who delivered nothing more than a brief precis on farm animals. None of us had farm animals so we left as ignorant as we arrived and a good deal more confused. Just to be safe, we all swore off kissing, holding hands and sitting in a seat after a boy. The distinction between Drugs and Medicines was never defined because it was completely unnecessary for anyone to know in *that kind of street.*

METAMORPHOSIS

Franz Kafta's Metamorphosis,
the story of salesman Gregor Samsa
who wakes one morning
to the shocking reality that he has morphed
into a huge insect, details a transformation
far less shocking than Mum's transformation
from mother to Peter and I, to grandmother.

Mum belted my brother and I
for crimes and misdemeanours
that would've been overlooked
in Oliver Twist's poorhouse. She
once sent us out to the backyard
to source a suitable weapon
for punishment. Apparently
we'd pushed her patience 'beyond
the pale, and she'd tired of ever
making anything of us, the pair of us
being hell bent on remaining heathens'.

I chose a thin stick. 'No. NO,'
said Peter, clearly more familiar
with this torturous system,
new to my tender experience. My next
choice, a thick plank was also vetoed.
'Leave it to me, sis,' he said.
For myself, I didn't see much difference
from the precious luggage strap
as I screamed blue murder.

"Nannie" would rather take a Valium than
lay a hand on a child, certainly not on Boy,
who ruled the kingdom with smiling requests
and stern, but gently delivered lectures
for her general edification and improvement.

What
did we fight over before television?
my brother and I never fought
Over the telly. He had seniority
a status I never thought to overthrow,
although I did whinge about the superfluity
repetitive formulaic inanity of Westerns.

The Boy tolerated school
school tolerated The Boy.
The Boy attended school, although
it can reliably be stated that The Boy
didn't make his mark there. On
the whole, he annoyed teachers
and teachers annoyed him. In order
to decrease the stultifying discomfort
of his formal education, The Boy
arrived at that institution as late
as he could manage without drawing
unwanted attention. The Boy
had to get himself off to school. I worked
the morning shift (7-3:30) at the local
nursing home 5 minutes away. Mothers
are expected to be everywhere. Single
mothers are expected to be everywhere
and then some.

The Boy had been late for a week.
by some nefarious means, now forgotten.
I realised he was watching telly
in the mornings. I gave the usual
parental lecture...'never again, you hear me'.

Full to the eyebrows of his own importance,
along with the accumulated significance
of past warlords, conquerors and kings,
The Boy boldly said, 'You can't make me.'

In the nurses staffroom the next day,
I sold the telly to whomever would
take it far, far away in the lunch hour.
Television gone.

That afternoon, The Boy brought
reinforcements to the fray—Nannie
sat beside him inside the door
in my immediate path
when I arrived home. Twin
warriors with folded arms
and that most tormenting weapon
of all, wounded silence. After
a cheery hello, I whistled
in the kitchen, feigning the ignorance
of The Sublimely Oblivious, knowing
my mother had the self-control
of a pit bull when a piece of her mind
was busting to be shared.

'How dare you,' she said. 'How
dare you dispose of the television
without consulting that boy.' She
pointed at him in case I'd forgotten
who he was. "That boy" continued
the pained silence saga
with the fortitude that comes
with childhood, where the only

goal in life is to get what they want.
After all, bills and life expenses
are not present to enlighten or deflect.

'When that boy pays half my mortgage,
he'll get a vote,' I said, feeling clever, but
doubting that I'd scored any points
anywhere but in my own head.

NANAS ARE NOT ICE-CREAM

If Boy wanted to see Nannie
spend time with her
he saw her. She loved him
with a tireless, extravagant love.
a love that peeved me to my toes
with its constant undermining
of my motherhood. But
Nanas are not ice-cream,
treats to be denied, withheld,
measured incrementally.

I challenged her, upbraided,
scolded, harangued, reproved.
It didn't change a jot. I dreamed
of escape to a quiet, coastal village
where the struggling single mother
makes a dozen friends overnight
and has a handsome neighbour
waiting to nurture someone else's child.
Very Mills & Boon and totally bonkers.

She loved him, with a tenacious
devotion, as if he was the gift
life had denied her, the summation
of her dreams. All the affection
that she'd been denied,
and the affection she'd withheld
from her own children
was found in a small boy
whose adoration was complete.

I AM WOMAN

I've used all my polite words
I've used all my slight words
my try-to-please,
not fright words
And I'm done.

With those soft explanations
those long expositions
and repeated justifications
for your elucidation
when you ask me why I do this. Why
I do that, why here, why there...?

So I'm done
with the limp words
the carefully crafted
politically correct
emotionally reduced
terminally inadequate
rhetoric.

I clutch my keys tighter
lock the car faster
park near street lights
shudder at shadows
stand with my back to the wall
choose my place fastidiously
on trains, buses and trams
I take no dark shortcuts
I move through the world
differently—
I have a vagina.

PLEASE SHUT UP

It's not about you, so please shut up

I've noticed of late a burgeoning trend
of focus on issues that make the mind bend
I'm speaking here of domestic violence
Now, grateful we are, for the breaking of silence
to no longer be told, 'Please shut up.'

But there's shame and disgrace in the tense debate
fuelled by statistics and dialogue in the ABC of late
some choose to view this new revelation as some kind
of war on christianity, church and all godly mankind
telling ABC journos to 'Please shut up.'

So if you're a smug man sitting in your snug seat
with high-minded opinions you're wont to repeat
taking umbrage at news that defines a real situation
that you've never experienced, no matter your vocation
It's not about you, so 'Please shut up.'

And yes, it's the women with slippers and soup
who've never been abused or thrown for a loop
by a man with such rage he'd throttle you dead
for undermining his God-given right as The Head
I'll include you too, 'Please shut up.'

Thank God for the outrage
bless those with the courage
the silence is broken
brave words have been spoken
it's not about you, so 'Please shut up.'

BEHIND WHISPERING HANDS

Behind whispering hands
lie seeds of suspicion
nurtured through the soil
of discontent
and spread
like midnight shrouds
unchecked

Behind whispering hands
in the womb
sheltered from the world
words begin in secret flutterings
draw tentative breath
and become
other

Behind whispering hands
lies become fact
twisting and turning
reaching beyond truth
grow, then fly
travel undeterred
afar

QUEEN OF CARAMEL COURT

As much as a bee hive
needs a queen bee,
every block of units
needs a queen. Good luck
staying on the throne if someone
of superior persistence
arrives, unpacks the removal boxes
hangs the drapes, sashays
past your door, and welcomes you.
It's her neighbourhood
now.

They'll ask when
it was that she won
and the answer will be
the moment she breezed
through the door
caring less
than everyone else.

She could sell
a homeless man
an engagement ring,
and he'd thank her
for a 25 year instalment plan
then kiss her feet.

She'll advise
about your hubby,
listen to your marital woes,

and just to prove
the depth of her loyal friendship,
she'll shun his advances. At least
for a while.

She presides over worker-bees
with their busy adoration. Over
drones with their willing
subjugation. For
brief hope of conjugation. With their
quivering pollen legs. Their
noisy wings,
their hum

Sole proprietor of pheromones
she smoothly decides
who's in
who's out

Allowing other females
into the hive
is a generosity she's willing to allow
within the rules. These
need no overt articulation—
temporary banishment,
or the chill of distance sees to that.
You may lend money,
bring tokens of devoted adoration,
 and when she says,
'Don't you think so?', all you have to do
is agree.

Hive queen will ghost you if you fall foul
of her benevolent regard, she's too kind
to confront. Face to face so 1990s.
It might take a while for the penny
to drop. She is gatekeeper, warden
of your wax-celled hive exile, far
from the tightly controlled,
guarded queendom.

Acutely attuned to sounds, hive queen
hears coins clink, paper money
crackle from at least a hundred yards
away—Here she comes now
swinging the pollen basket
dancing her slow dance
vibrating antennae

                              seeking royal jelly.

SHOE LEATHER

Put some shoe leather on your prayers
put some shoe leather on your promises.
if the supplications on your knees
are more acquisition than contrition
it's not a prayer with shoe leather
if I'm on your list for divine attention
yet you can't walk through my door
here, there, or somewhere there's a flaw
if your religion resembles The Secret
with its Amway-like focus on prosperity
you don't have much in common
with the man who wore out shoe leather
and surrendered to suffering.

How dare you preach abundance
as God's will for all his children?
you'll bring thousands to believe
thousands ready to receive
thousands to the coffers
for the wages, for the proffers
and the prosperous will praise you
the crowds will adore you
the meek will implore you
and seek to be like you.

But what about the wheelchairs
that are never abandoned, never
thrown aside with jubilation?
What about the cancers that cling
rip and tear and prevail?

What about the humble seekers
where suffering doesn't recede
before your tide of mighty healing?
what about them?

You think you're offering
a better life, a triumph measured
scrupulously by the faith on offer,
sought and bought, purchased
and secure, a fortress against
a world of suffering—but

all that high-ceilinged praise, the glory
of the choral contribution, the velvet
of the offering bags, the carefully
coiffed confection of your presentational
perfection only offers one thing
for those stumbling through disease,
loss and poverty.
Guilt.

You're selling the supreme
originally crafted deceptive lie
you shall not surely die. Because
all suffering is a mini death.

THE FLIES ON YOUR WALL...

The flies on your wall have been talking. You didn't
see them, didn't notice their vibrations. Their silent
flutterings. In the corners of the safe secret places
of your walls. You don't think I know. It's not even
that you've probed my broken pieces. Or that you
decried my midnight angst. You think I deserve it
deserve it all, chose it. And you're coming. To give
voice to the words you've hidden, from me. You're
packing, folding with precision, your clothes, your
words. 'Sorry if ... things on my mind'. All precisely
rehearsed as your itinerary. You don't think I know.

WAR

Rupture of earth
roar of cannon
battlefield banners
brutal tear of body and blue serge
brass buttons
on the blood-stained ground
Hate has a new visage
an old face on a young man

death's surprised, cold stare
caught unawares
no greater insanity
war

It's just a telemovie
Isn't it?
rain of metal
magazine empties
into the crowd
guns,
automatic assault
faster, better, smarter
with each technical evolution
crueller, more cunning
than the last

Hate has a new visage
Flash of light
Staccato rhythm
Pa rat tat ta ta

'I thought it was the music'
Tympanum vibrato
'Goodbye Mum'

Death's surprised, cold stare
caught unawares
no greater insanity
peace

Hate has a new visage
the manic anger
of a politician
his hate larger, more brutal
than his accused

No greater insanity
Politics

UNFAITH-FUL

Lucretia watches him with almond eyes. He stares.
Unblinking, solid, frozen, wounded. Measuring
the space between them she advances,
feet softly padding, sinuous curving of a feline.

For three days she wraps herself around his pain
willing him to forget her prowling indiscretion
her arched-back love-making against the rough tree.

Mewling soft sounds against his taut throat
have replaced screaming protestations.

Unfurling one long leg, she surrounds him
thigh against naked thigh. But
he's neutral, mind fug too dense to penetrate.

Her thin tattered camisole slips from a shoulder.
firm rounded breasts caress bunching bicep
as she traces the dragon tattoo down his arm
gazing up through mascara-smudged eyes
her silken hair trapped in his five o'clock shadow
lush hair falling, shading tear stained lies.

She winds herself around him
with timed perfection
his thumb rubs her palm, she purrs a sigh
retribution to forgiveness
not one word spoken.

OPUS OF RAGE

(Trigger warning—themes of family violence)

I

He waits in tense silence, hearing the stumbling footfall on the doorstep then muffled cursing as a key jars in the lock.

His father is home.

He is fourteen years old, his lanky body taut as he slides from his bed to stand at the bedroom door, his head bent, leaning into the darkness. He stretches muscles that are tight from helping his mother with her evening cleaning job. It keeps food on the table.

The sound of grinding gears woke him minutes earlier.

He's a light sleeper, a restless one, with the honed instincts of a soldier. Attune to the night, he listens. He fights an electric prickle of anxiety, waiting for the signs that are precursor to violence.

Violence threads through his days, even while his athletic body finds release in sport, basketball, soccer, cross country. Violence taints his nights, even the quiet ones—those somnolent stretches of peace. Because there is always a shadow. A shadow that thunders, retreats and returns.

He winces at the sound of clattering in the kitchen. He moans, tonight won't be one of those nights his father passes out on the couch. *Stay in your room, Mum*—his silent prayer. He doesn't understand why she pleads, placates or why she sometimes fights back. There is no way to comprehend why the walls of this house shape the construct of the most dangerous place he's ever known.

The police come often.

His father hurls abuse at them with democratic ease.

A scraping, shuffling noise tells him one of the younger ones has been woken and is going to the toilet. His hands clench.

He hears his mother's soft voice to the child, and prays his father won't hear. In vain.

It begins—the dense drama that is family life.

'Why can't you make those children obey you?'—the opening prelude to the opus of rage.

He steps into the hallway. Hate radiates from the man in front of him, he is both stranger and father.

Fast, angry and drunk, his father strikes.

The younger children are all awake now, screaming, whimpering; clawing at their mother's nightie.

He towers over his stocky father.

Once his mere presence was enough to stop the onslaught, but not anymore. Once he merely protected, now he is aggressor.

'You're as bad as me,' his father roars.

In the morning they will work side by side, hammering, planning, building.

Each in their own silence.

He will respect and honour his father. In the morning.

But tonight he's measuring blow for blow.

He vows, *I'll never be like you.*

OPUS OF RAGE

II

He paces the upstairs kitchen.

He's stressed. It's been a tough week. No one seems to understand the pressure of trying to teach dozens of kids, no one in this house anyway.

Not the people under his own roof. Not the woman he married after his divorce, the one who soothes and coddles her own son, as well as the baby she has borne to him. The son he dreamed of, a son to carry his name.

His wife is breastfeeding the baby now, cooing and caressing the infant's downy head. He doesn't know why but this affection grates.

'I wish you wouldn't demand feed,' he says, his voice rising. 'I don't agree with it. *On demand*, who does that? Don't you see? Kids who are demand fed are spoiled.'

He fumes. He should be the head of the house.

And as for that boy, *her* fourteen year old son, the kid shows *no* respect. To anyone. The boy's surly silences infuriate, prickle and crawl under his skin, eating at him, taunting him.

He'd rather open rebellion, heated exchanges than this, this voiceless insolence. This arrogant obedience.

He approaches her, his anger fermenting. 'I sent that kid down to tidy the garage. What's taking him so long?'

'Maybe he doesn't know where to put your tools, your things,' she says. 'It's chaos down there.'

He stabs at her with a finger. 'I'm too busy to run a house as well as a school.' His voice is gritty, resentful.

He stands at the top of the stairs and calls the boy.

'Makes my blood boil,' he mutters, clenching his teeth.

He is greeted with silence, then a shuffling sound, feet scraping. The sounds of reluctance, defiance. The stairwell amplifies the sound.

55

He waits.

His blood is heating. She's oblivious, sitting in the lounge that backs on to the stair railing. Still petting the baby. She'll ruin the kids, both of them. Turn them into sappy spoilt brats.

He watches as the boy begins his slow ascent. He launches into a blistering tirade.

The boy says nothing, not even when he is standing on the step below him.He lands a full body blow that spills the boy down the stairs. He follows, roaring and punching. Then kicking as the boy lies still. He rains blows, vision blurred, control gone.

'Why don't you fight like a man?' he rages.

The boy whispers, *I'll never be like you.*

Then the man hears his wife scream, endless piercing that fractures the air. He runs back up the stairs to her.

'I only stopped hitting *that boy* because I heard you scream and thought you'd dropped MY son!'

She freezes.

He rants. He speaks of righteous indignation, of respect, of obedience.

Then leaves, taking the phone and the car.

Placing the baby down with care, she runs down the stairs, heart pounding, calling her son's name. Unaware that she'd screamed, she wonders if her son is alive. She finds him, pale, cold and bleeding. Bruised and crouching.

She weeps.

She weeps for wounds she can never heal, for a heart that cannot be unbroken. For a son who will wear the scars of battle. From a man she brought into his life.

She weeps for a son who will cross the bridge to manhood with a tainted, seared psyche. She attends to him.

She finds a public phone. They don't take teenage boys at the refuge. It's a new town, she knows no one. Isolation and fear claw at her stomach.

She moves in a fog.

When he returns he is still fermenting.

He strides the house with primal rage. He is livid, they have no idea how far they've pushed him, what they have made him become. He demands respect.

She pleads softly to take the boys and stay with her mother, 'just for a few days, to let everyone heal, get past things'.

He spins to face her. 'Walk out that door and I'll take my son, and you'll never see him again.'

The air is taut with menace.

He turns to glare at the boy who is standing in the corner, then slides his eyes to her.

'You won't find me, but I'll find you. Then no one else will find you.'

The boy learns deeper silence.

It's a habit he'll take into manhood.

I'll never be like you.

FIRST CRIES

first cries
break pale moon streaming
lungs raw at first contact
querulous crescendo
bereft of womb comfort
the die cast for
life

pale pre-dawn
struggling
into bright light
fresh hope

pink lips
seek tiny fists
blue eyes' myopic focus
finds mother, father
their hearts stretched
beyond understanding
as vulnerable in this moment
as their newborn child

I touch the sticky flush
of your face
bright eyes
take first sight
fingers grasp
babe of my child
but strangely my own

THE GRIEF

I had an elderly patient
who lived in a rundown shack
in the scrub
the louvered windows rattled
the doors stuck.

We community nurses
had been visiting
for over a year,
without improvement
to a leg ulcer.

The meat in his fridge
had maggots
a spectacular feat
in anyone's books.

After I dressed his leg
I'd sit and chat,
accept a cup of tea, served
on a clean cloth
on a grubby table.

'I had THE GRIEF,'
he said one day, donating
capital letters
and gravitas to sorrow.

'Near did me in, it did.'

THE IDEA OF YOU

I don't know if I mourn you
or the idea of you
    you are gone
my grief is tangible
I mourn a void, a definable loss
    but it's not an ache
for missed brunches, catchups
lost holidays
    or even absence
the thought that catches
and teases
sullen corners of my mind
    you didn't know me
I didn't know you
no matter how many
escarpments I climbed
I didn't find you
    who erected the barriers?
did I? did you?
    was it just a tragic farce?
of bad timing, myopic memory
or geography?

all I know—I sit alone
grieving a question
for the answer has scattered on the wind
    perhaps the same wind
that carried the ash
of your earthly unbeing

    and all that is left for me—
to mourn the idea of you

MEMOIR FOR MY SON
(Trigger warning—themes of suicide, depression)

I can't let you
disappear
in death,
the way you
disappeared
in life.

That's why
I'm here,
breaking
my heart
all over again.

WITHOUT ARMOUR

I am without armour;
living my life
on the outside
of my skin.

It's a hard day,
today. I shouldn't
write on a hard day.
I should write
on a better day, a more
pulled-myself-together day,
but then, perhaps
I should write
on whatever day I'm having
so I'm writing today.

My son
took his own life
on July 9, 2019.

He sorted all his things,
leaving the least amount
of pain he could.
left a letter, 'Sorry Mum,
then his children's names...
in order.

He blamed no one,
ending with, 'I'm going home,
where God can heal
his broken child.'

I cannot tell you
how much I miss him.
I miss him with every breath.

All his life he wanted
to be a hero to his family.
That doesn't mean
he was a hero in suicide
undertaking a heroic act.
It doesn't mean he left me
though God knows
I could argue that point
a thousand different ways.
He left his life.
He left himself.

I'm angry at times. Yesterday
I drove past Krispy Cremes, bawled
like a baby and said, 'You'll never
have another Krispy Crème,
did you think of that, you silly boy?'

Yet all the meanings of my heart
are best summed up with
'How do I go on without
one of the brightest
lights of my life?'

After his wife left
with his three children
he attempted suicide,

then
after talking
his way out
of the mental health unit
he messaged me
with his usual sparsity of words:
"u there mum?

He arrived off the plane
in Op Shop clothes
with a suitcase of tattered
childhood mementos
and a few of his children's' toys
that had been left behind
in the empty house.

He was introverted,
thoughtful,
deep, flawed.
Shadowed
by inner pain,
not
tormented
by inner demons

He had been living with me,
struggling and falling.
deeper

He turned everything inward,
a lifetime habit.

He had been with me
for nearly three years.
I was always afraid.
I'd been afraid throughout
His father's suicide events,
and feared...
I became more afraid
as the lawyers bartered.

This for that,
3 days access
bargained down to three hours
(with 30 days notice)

by a pert young thing
with trendy, blonde bi-tresses
and a legal resume that read
like an online dating profile
who spelled her name in court
in case the judge was senile.
B. U. R. N. S.

An intense young father
with his lists, dates, papers and facts
quiet serious demeanour
and precise, quiet words
couldn't compete
with fast fancy footwork.

THE PORCH LIGHT

is flicking
on and off,
as if by some unseen
trigger.

It bathes
the destitute lounge room
in piercing light
then retreats.
it will return,
but you will not.
gone,
forever,
vanquished.

death's cold kiss
upon your face.
I can't bring you back.

I never want
to sleep again,
for you will be there
in my dreams, wriggling
the end of the bed,
asking if I want to go
for pizza,
or Subway,
to the Thai place
or Marvel movies.

but
then I'll wake and
it will hit and smash and tear.

And I'll remember
that you're gone.

your jacket comforts me.
it has the scent of you.
a few molecules of you.
all I have
or ever will.

I'll grasp that scent
breathe it in,
as I wish I'd been able
to breathe life
back into you,
your huge lungs,
now empty.

When will I
wake?
When will I
live without you?
Without
your tender concern
for
funny little mother.

Your last letter to me,
"Sorry mum...

No place

I can't sit in a court
and speak my pain
at your act,
for my loss.

there's no place for my
victim statement
no place for me
to accuse
despise
decry
this violence
this theft of a life.

because
you
threw it away.

I'm failing

at past tense.

'I love him so much'
refuses
to become
"loved"
because my love
hasn't gone
just
because you have.

my body
was your first home
my heart
your first pulse.
How close to my heart
was the warm cave
where you grew.
safe as long as I
was safe.

When you were born,
you hesitated
before you breathed
as if deciding
whether to join this world
or to leave
before the madness
began.

And even though
you're dead
and my heart
doesn't understand
the strange act of beating
without you in this world,
I'm glad you took
that first breath
and stayed, giving
me some of the purest
happiest moments
of my life.

I'm waiting
for the sentimental music
the slowly falling petals
the pristine lilies
that exemplify
death
in the movies.

DOUBT

Doubt
walked in
unpacked a few suitcases
hung a few suits
rearranged a few rooms
to suit itself

checked where everything
was kept
checked if there
was enough
of everything

looks like it's come
to stay awhile
welcome or not

it's not.

I guess it came
for the empty room

after all
certainty left
with you.

EXIST

They tell me you no longer
exist. That you've evaporated
like the steam from a kettle.

No matter how I try
I simply can't get my head
around that rationality.

I know every response
you'd give, every joke you'd get,
every angst you'd feel.

I know that you're not
here. Here with me, softly
shuffling through my days.

But who you were is constant. My
love for you unchanged, undimmed,
irrationally extravagantly present.

To grieve a man means a woman
can love another. To grieve a son
is to grieve the irreplaceable.

Although you were cleaved
from my life, my love has grown
around the fallen trunk.

And thus I go on. A strange,
transmuted growth, embracing
what was, existing in this world.

I FORGIVE YOU

it's okay
I forgave you
in the very first moment.

I Will

I will not
wander
off
into the dark
night
from whence
came
my sorrow.

I will
be fierce.

I will be
present.

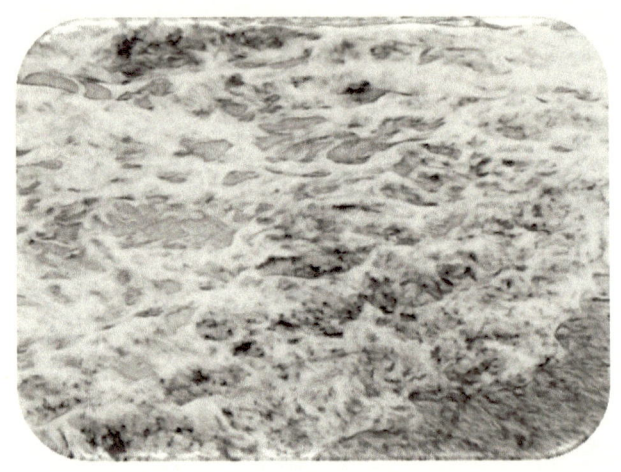

DOVES FALL

doves fall
peace dies
brittle hearts
cold stone
buried guilt
false shame

muted innocence
muffled voice
cruel burden
harsh crime

soft tears
wrenched choice
crossed purposes
twisted lines
subtle whisper
sharp intent

listen now
light flickers
joy flutters
hope shines

divine comes

BEAUTY

Singing whales far away glide in the deep
furry creatures in forests scurry and creep
bats fly high, hang upside down
heedless of people, country or town

A slow drifting moon reigns in the sky
Southern Cross stars suspended up high
tall trees shudder, bend in pale moonlight
while I discern sombre songs of the night

BLESSED BE

Blessed be the dream makers
the early morning bakers
the givers among the takers

Blessed by the truth sifters
the burden lifters
the sorrow shifters

Blessed be the rhythm groovers
the heavy-liftin' house removers
those every-day manoeuvres

Blessed be those who wait
those who silently anticipate
those who willingly participate

TO LOVE

The lights in the corridor
are dim and low.
The evening shadows
have lengthened.
A frail woman lies quietly.
She hears not.
She sees blurry visions of life.
I have come to check her.

It is we two
alone
in the dark night.
I caress her face gently
before switching on the light.
She knows my touch.

Her face glows with a joy
I've rarely seen
in conquering heroes,
much less a bed-ridden
sparrow of a woman.

In all of what life throws me,
that look will always be
the measure of who I am.

SPACE IN A TIME OF COVID

No, I'm not talking Elon Musk and his swanky Dream Come True space odyssey. It's the supermarket. I'd been to Barossa Food Wonderland a few times in the time of Covid and found that all the customers and servers were social distancing as if they were in the Russian Ballet. All natural grace, and polite nodding. Until today.

A checkout woman past the classification of 'chick' was serving customers with all the gusto of a philharmonic conductor and repeating, 'Social Distancing, please,' as if she just discovered the words and was so enamoured with their poetic beauty that she had to repeat the phrase frequently, along with an extravagant gesture that would have made goat herders weep with envy.

I approached and began to stack my items on the conveyor noting that her current customer was a two metres away at the end of the line packing items into her trolley. The checkout woman was a slow as a wet week, even though they don't seem as slow as they once did.

She wasn't watching the items as they passed over the blipper as she was heavily engaged in conversation with the customer who was about ten inches from her as they shared their pain at not being able to make use of the brand new caravans purchased pre-Covid, 'if only we'd known.' They sounded as if they were lifelong friends but may have only just met – supermarkets are like that. One had aborted a trip to Darwin, the other had a yen for The Peninsula.

The items passed the scanner, the scanner blipped, goodness knows how many of the items were missed or scanned twice. Checkout woman noticed me, 'Social Distancing, please,' she said, waving her arm with the snide smirk of a rental evictor.

I rolled the milk bottles onto the conveyor.

She rolled her eyes.

A woman in the queue behind me moved forward.

Checkout woman waved an imperious arm and repeated 'Social Distancing, please,' until the poor woman was halfway down the pet food aisle. The two at the end continued their dissertation on travel-hunger in a time of Covid. The customer had blue ticking bags with strange white strings attached. Checkout woman struggled with these contraptions and broke one of the dangling strings before loading another bag. She then asked, 'Would you like the rest of your items bagged?'

I stared at the two pineapples on the conveyor belt and made a rough guess that the woman didn't want to carry them out of the shop under her arm.

By this time the customer halfway down the pet food aisle had galloped off to another line and was heading for the carpark.

A gentleman in a wheelchair approached the line. 'Social Distancing, please,' she informed him. He looked at the woman then at the controls. I don't think he'd thoroughly conquered reverse. He stared at a can he was holding then at the conveyor belt.

'Any good at basketball?' I enquired politely.

'Social Distancing, please,' said Madam Checkout, clearly aiming for a position in management or government. When I finally arrived at the checkout, the daft woman leaned forward to get my card.

It took all my self-control to refrain from—'Social Distancing, please.'

THOSE SMALL FICTIONS

There were
no funeral arrangements,
no place to lay flowers,
nowhere to mark
a son's life and passing
lost to war

If at all, those ceremonies
had been hastily performed far away,
on alien soil.

The sisters
walk the cemetery rows,
stopping
      here
and there,

remembering
other lost loved ones
and creating
those small fictions,
those alternate memories
that comfort and sustain the bereaving.

SILENCES

We thought there was a bridge
spanning the space between. But
our connection to each other
we built on silences

On each side of the divide
we both strained our reach. But
across the mist and darkness
we built on silences

Halfway across the breach
with all the right intentions. But
we started out in different places
we built on silences

Guessing and assumptions
were grand and nobly sought. But
how could we meet across the chasm
we built on silences

And now as I am reaching
I'm hoping for your voice. But
you need to know I'm listening
nothing is built on silences

WHAT THEY DID NEXT...

Thomas Hardy as a motivational speaker
Jane Eyre sets up a psychic centre
Hemingway preaches sobriety
Romeo becomes a paid escort

Rochester teaches anger management
Mrs Dalloway counsels for Lifeline
Byron as a hairdresser
Poe studies to be a mortician

Oliver Twist becomes a pudding magnate
Tolstoy takes up mime and flash fiction
Macbeth as a sales rep for hospital-grade cleansing
agents
Sykes as a human rights lawyer

Mary Lennox starts a pesticide company
Mr Bennet cultivates a strain of tea with sedative effects
Kipling as an all-hours pharmacist
Richard III sets up a preschool and day care centre

RAIN

Rain arrives sideways, on an erratic,
busy wind. It's a wind with a deadline. It rushes
through gaps around the front door, as if
it's been to many places and has many yet to visit.
It flies straight in. It's a big blouse wind,
a full frontal confident blast, no insidious
gap-slipping manoeuvres, like a relative
who's never been quelled, put in their place.

In my last house the chill crept in
with secret intent, seeped beyond
yellowed gap filler – hardened
from the scorch of sunny days. It brought
a careful rain, slipping past silicone barriers

like water through teeth, leaving surprise
puddles on large square tiles. And
outside, it was shiftier—eroding earth
under pavers, leaking
into underground ag-pipe canals,
silting into the cavern of the stormwater

drain at the front of the house. The one
that collapsed two years ago, taking
torn shards of tarred road, like
broken chocolate, but not taking my car.

A neighbour,
a real worry-wart had told me
not to park there —'Your car
will end up in China', she said.

I shifted the car, just to keep her happy.
Her hyper-vigilance amused me, and besides,
she made a great coffee. When the road
caved in we stood either side
of the modest sink-hole and nodded wisely.

Too Much (Thinking of You)

It's 2 or 3 o'clock in the morning. But
I'm superstitious about checking the time.
It will prejudice me about how tired to feel
at dawn. I'm sitting here, reading Dorothy
Parker's poem, ambiguously titled Resume,
the one that begins 'Razors pain you'
thinking of the mix of humour and angst.
The comic and tragic that the Greeks
call farce. Or was it Shakespeare?

I'm wondering how you are. But I don't
want to know. It's always been an odd thing.
I'm supposed to be the caller, while
your role was always the callee, ready
to castigate me if I left it too long. Never
thinking to pick up the phone. Some
relationships are like that, balanced
precariously on a piano wire. Just
like you were, all those years ago. When
you flirted with the precipice. Tiptoed

to the edge of life. Seeing if suicide
might fit better than what you had
a part-time marriage with a man
too afraid to leave, too departed to
stay. Balanced on his own indecision,
caught, not between you and his lover
but between the other woman
and himself. While you clawed at him
drowning for his dead love.

I remember that conversation on that most
ordinary day. The strangeness of it all. The
disconnected brutality of its perambulation
and my balancing act between horror
and confusion. You'd made cupcakes, with
pink frosting. And silver buttons. We sat
companionably in your pristine kitchen while
our tots playing in the next room—Travis!
don't get any more Lego out,' you said,

'there's enough mess in there!' And then—
'I'm just out of hospital you know. I tried
to kill myself, pills of course. That's
the easiest way. Although if one was
desperate enough' ... then a sudden shift—
'Would you like another cupcake? Sugar
with your tea? A nice choccy biccie. I
have plenty—You said all that, while
nibbling on all those delights, while

I choked on your words. And couldn't find
any of my own. They'd died on my lips,
between tea, cake and despair. I looked
out of the window. It looked like a normal
day. The sun was shining. Your clothes
hung on the line. In perfect lineation
as they always did. But where were you?
Did you fathom the carnage of your words?
My four year old son went and sat in the car—
'What's the matter with him?' you said.

Inside my head I was screaming. It's wrong—
this is a conversation for a blacker day,
a blustering chaotic day. Not a zesty, spring-
rejoicing noon. There should be a storm
outside—shrieking, impotent with rage, not
this. This filtered sunlight on a pristine table
fine bone coffee cups between us. I can't do this,
I thought. I can't be your one-man-band.

The fear-stiffened banner-waver, mute
at your suicide parade. 'I'll do it one day—
don't tell...' you whispered into my trembling.
But your secret was too tight to hide in me. In
the broken vessel of my own tears. Your pain
was bigger, fiercer, more epic than my weapons.
Your raw-death sweet-freedom vows broke me
too. I couldn't be your solution. Your 'stop me'

resolution while your other friends. Your
laugh-out-loud good-time crowd didn't even
suspect your secret sting, so, I'm thinking about
you. I'm wondering how you are. But I don't
want to know. It's always been an odd thing.

WEAVER

the heddle has fallen
the loom lays bare
yesterday's bright threads
strewn without care

no whirr of the shuttle
no more picking or shedding
no plain, twill or satin
no battening or beating

but here in the village
time has a different claim
the weaver's swift rhythm
is a mystic refrain

FEAR

Hit me
and I will fear you

Hit me
and tell me you love me
and I will fear love

Never knowing if I deserve it
carrying a gnawing hunger
to possess it

Living in shadows
left with a void
I must fill
because you cannot

KITCHEN TABLE

At our last parting
you gave me your stories
I gave you mine. I gave you
my kitchen table and
you gave me yours. I see
grooves and shadows
where we often sat. Where
your family and friends
had broken bread
all those years.

I hear shades
of that laughter,
and those tears. There
are scratches
on your table, and mine
grooved markings
of the written word,
yours, theirs
mine.

Friendship, the word
isn't sufficient
wide enough or wonderful enough
for the manner of loyalty and respect
you gave as instinctively
as breathing. You put
your feet under my table.

You broke bread
at my table. And you stayed,
stayed until
you declared my favourite chair
should be renamed
as the 'bad back chair'. You
stayed. Anything else
isn't friendship.

God bless those who love enough
to break bread. Those
who care sufficiently
to put their feet
under our tables. Those
who sit and trace
the grooves of life
and friendship.

CORNER TABLE

Winter's blast enters with me
slamming the glass door to the café
you're already here, pretending
not to wait, holding your gaunt frame erect

You move when you see me, stepping
forward with careful pace, waving
a pale tight-skinned hand, choosing
the table in a sunlit corner

You've aged twenty years in two, so thin
you almost fold in half. Wanting
information on the cancer, I lean in to hope
I didn't get the email attachment, I say

The left corner of your mouth jerks
the way it always has. You release
a deep sigh, then details: biopsies
mesothelioma, late stages, medications, prognosis

You accept the coffee, declining
the menu with minimal gesture, then
frown as I place gold coins on the table
I don't want ... anything, you say

We don't notice the ten am rush as
we measure our words
with resolute precision, stalling
and starting, clinging to script

You disappear into the street, drowning
in the traffic, leaving
me to walk the other way
I wish you'd let me say goodbye.

THE UNSAME

When I was young
I watched Slavic women with headscarves
hurry from the store, heads bowed, eyes down
not wanting to see, not wanting to know
how the others, the undifferent,
viewed them, appraised them.

How different they were, scurrying about
different food, different language
taking children out of school
to visit the doctor, the solicitor, the bank.
the biggest difference, their struggle,
their isolation,
recipients of our scrutiny
objects of pity and shame.

How ridiculous it seems now.

We move on
we cycle our disdain
recycle our enemies
from some distant high tower–
gays, then races, religions and creeds
the Triads, the African gangs, Lebanese mobs, the Mafia
with nary a thought or media release about "Aussies"
our gangs, our crimes, our belligerent hate.
No, not us, we'd never be THAT
never be "those people"
those miscreants.
We're mates!

High church and low church
crosses or nay, ornaments or frugality
rich-robed or fine-suited, dirges or praise.
We judged them all.

Every group judged by the actions of one.

So many words for speech
I'm so tired of the semantic, the expert conjecture
the discussion, the "information sharing".
Do we need more conversation than rhetoric?
more listening than rabble rousing,
opinion and debate?

As a teen I was confused by gayness
I read books, watched telly, desiring to understand.
Discussed, asked questions,
heard opinion and debate.

I needed an electrical appliance
some complicated annoying thing.
Terry served me, spent time, lots of time, explaining
ordering, adjusting, installing, with humour and grace.
I never knew what people-centred customer service was
before meeting Terry. Warm, witty efficient as hell.

I didn't need to understand gayness
anymore. I knew Terry.
So I judged all by the one.

We hated the Germans, then put away
our guns and bought their watches.

We hated the Japanese, then put away
our bombs and went to their expos.
We hated the Lebs, Chinese and Italians
then elected them to parliament.
(Thank God for that!)

The questions don't matter
nearly as much when we take those steps closer,
look into the eyes, hear the stories, break bread
with the dispossessed, the minority
the different, the unsame.

Like the Slavic women of my childhood
most are frightened and alone
out of country and home
relying on us, their neighbour, for place
not so unsame
at all.

ANNIVERSAIRE SOLITAIRE

I have been solo for longer than I've been spousally coupled. People feel pity for this diminished state, often saying, "Haven't you found a man?" to which I characteristically reply, "Can't they find themselves?" It's usually an attempt to get them off the subject and works, as humour often does...

Like many girls I dreamed of princely mannered men on sleek white steeds, wooing and cooing at the marvel of "me". But someone must have shot the horse, then the prince's shoes pinched, his feet blistered, thus making a longish journey impossible and a nearer female a more promising proposition.

So I wondered. If I had been thusly chosen, wooed and won – who would I be?

Would I have been valeted wherever I went? Jetted afar? Accustomed to fine dining, hotels and holiday destinations that didn't involve relatives? Organising maids? Rostering "the help"?

And yet ... would I have known the charity queue, the pawn shop modus operandi? Would I have been picking dressmaking pins off the floor, late for dinner, again? Would I have given up on tradespersons and done the jobs myself, an inept apprentice to no one but YouTube? Would I have parked too close to the exits on night duty, travelled doors locked, on alert? Checking the dark house when I arrived home? Would I have written a manifesto to the Bank, titled "Frugality: The Lost Art" in order to get a loan, alone? Would I have been playing in the gutter with mud to my knees, watching my son chase a frog, while peas and carrots burned on the stove?

Would I have drawn emus and cassowaries in the light of the telly? Would I have moved furniture around until it drove my sons nuts? Would I have painted fruit on cabinets? Painted the house, room by room, wall by wall with all the furniture on one side then on the other? Would I have used so much gap filler, spackle and silicone seal? Would I be ambidextrous with hammers and axes? Would I have taken my unwilling sons to see my work in the nursing home so they would know life? Would I have tied an inflatable boat to the roof of my tiny car, then paddled up Dora Creek with my son? Would I have made a miniature representation of Pilgrim's Progress on the loungeroom floor with cardboard and glue? Would I have perfected the art of scone-making instead of lumps that would service as garden rocks? Would I have learned "my place" as demure, circumspect?

Would I have lived and loved, laughed and cried the same way?

Would I have learned that: I am the bugler, I am the cavalry, I am the vanguard, the last troop in. I am the stockade and the watchman. Troops A through to Z with a hefty dose of "F Troop".

Last night I dreamed of palaces, coaches, men on white horses. Of paupers and thatch roofs, grimy fireplaces and wicker brooms. There was a handsome man whose interest I desired. He had a brown horse but I put that aside, as one does in dreams. He rode beautifully, off into the sunset with another.

Fleet-footed and young again, with flowing dark hair, I ran out of the thatched hut and cried at the injustice. There, in the courtyard, was a small white horse, stirruped and sadled, waiting. For me.

So thanks to the "princes" for riding on by, for choosing another more "suited" than I. Thanks to those heroes with superior bravado, telling me when and where to come and to go.

I'll raise a glass to an Anniveraire Solitaire, and to all my brave friends who join me there.

GARDEN

A hedonistic Hebe has gloried
in my somnolence, while my head-fug
has rushed like tidal seas
with new caplet salvation
from relentless tri-nerve intrusion.

A simple perfect budded-rose
has bloomed despite my absence, two weeks
without my fretting presence.
Striated Camellia beauty surprises on its
five-year birthday. Delinquent jonquils—
an early push through leaf-litter covers,
portending winter's chills
and the time when Lilac Cedar leafed abundance

will golden and fall. While near the city
of the veil of tears
still diamond-bright with memory,
a cohort of men of the ilk of Rasputin, follow
another tyrant, the horseman just-Putin
delivering a war for every generation
LIVE and streaming,
to threaten humanity's frail resources,
yet iron-willed resistance. Every mother, father
trembles. Grown sons and daughters
beyond the age of heeding, defend, protect.
Outside, the birds are gabbing gaily, inside
the politicians are blabbing daily.

I rise
and seek
the garden
once more.

WHEN I WAS SIX-SEVEN

When I was six-seven
I found a raven sleek
feathers blue-black
in morning-bright sunshine
lying sleep-peaceful, floating
lightly on leaf-bedded bliss
eyes dream tight-shut
among the weed-tall verge
of the choked-busy road.

I hoped;
I hoped for wakeful flight, but
no breath-movement
came or went, rose or sank.

Small legs push-pumping
speed-peddling my rattling bike
home.

Cardboard shoebox
repose for somnolence
I preened the raven—preserving
pristine perfection.

Father's bird-resting prayer
over soft-mounded earth.
I placed a flower-bright
sadly-teared, knowing
of future glory-withering.

Author

Linda Brooks lives in Adelaide. She has a BA Hons in Creative Writing. She gained a publisher for her childhood memoir 'A Curious & Inelegant Childhood'. She has written two books on Asperger's Syndrome with Professor Tony Attwood: *'I'm not broken, I'm just different'*, also published as *Don't read this book by my mother, she's crazy*, and *Callan the Chameleon*.

Published in anthologies: 'Coastlines' 5, 6, 7 & 8; 'Wood, Bricks & Stone'; 'Grieve' and 'Longing for Solitude'. Awards: Rebecca Coyle Scholarship for Hons; first prize for The Legacy University Level Creative Writing Award; first prize in the Gabe Reynaud Creative Writing Award and the Mater Misericordiae Grieve Writing Award.

Linda lives in Adelaide where she operates an online business *LRB Publishing Services* that assists authors with design and formatting. She occasionally helps with editing. Not often because she's rubbish at finding typos, especially her own.

Author titles

Nonfiction:
I'm not broken, I'm just different
(on Asperger's Syndrome with Professor Tony Attwood)
A Curious and Inelegant Childhood
Poetry:
Seeking the Sun Henry Kendall competition)
Third Wednesday Poets—an anthology

Adult fiction:
The day the war ended
Behind Whispering Hands
The Unprize
A broken hallelujah
Scarlett doesn't live here anymore
Under the Bracken Fern

Children's books:
A Tabby Never Forgets
An Angels Tears
Callan the Chameleon (Asperger's Syndrome)
Dusty Bunny's Very Important Job
Ethereal Land
Izzy & Pudding the Cat
I want a monkey!
Madam Iris Bigglesworth
The Frog that Hiccupped
When the stars move
Who Stole Christmas?

Publisher of the anthologies:
We are Australian'
The Great Australian Shed
Waltzing Matilda

www.ingramcontent.com/pod-product-compliance
Lightning Source LLC
Chambersburg PA
CBHW020530120726
47904CB00003B/1031